Dear Paul,
I hope you enjoy this.
I've enjoyed getting
to know you and I
plan to take full
advantage of your
wisdom and clear
thinking in the
next 2 years.
Enjoy —
David
5/27/06

Bella Donna

a dark comedy in two acts

Bella Donna

a dark comedy in two acts

by

David Copelin

Playwrights Canada Press
Toronto • Canada

Playwrights Canada Press
The Canadian Drama Publisher
215 Spadina Ave. Suite 230, Toronto, Ontario CANADA M5T 2C7
416.703.0013   fax 416.408.3402
orders@playwrightscanada.com • www.playwrightscanada.com

Financial support provided by the taxpayers of Canada and Ontario through the Canada Council for the Arts and the Department of Canadian Heritage through the Book Publishing Industry Development Programme, and the Ontario Arts Council.

Front cover sword © 2006 Jupiterimages Corporation
Cover design: David Copelin and JLArt
Production Editor: MZK

Library and Archives Canada Cataloguing in Publication

Copelin, David
    Bella Donna / David Copelin.

A play.
ISBN 0-88754-840-7

    1. Borgia, Lucrezia, 1480-1519—Drama.
2. Italy—History—1492-1559—Drama.
I. Title.

PS8555.O59292B44 2006   C812'.6   C2006-900048-4

First edition: March 2006.
Printed and bound by AGMV Marquis at Quebec, Canada.

for Sue Miner
with admiration, affection, and anticipation

Acknowledgements:

Thanks to the following artists, scholars, and institutions for their diverse contributions to *Bella Donna:*
Marion Adler, Starla Benford, Juan Chioran, Ann Ciccolella, Peggy Coffey, David Mark Cohen, Mary Coleman, Pamela Delaney & PostScript Productions, Elise Dewsberry, Kate Draper, Elizabeth English & Moondance International Film Festival, Rachel Erlanger, Andrea Fletcher, Rick Hickman & Upstart Stage, Kim Horsman, Victor Hugo, Greg LeGros, Anika Johnson, Lin Joyce & Equity Showcase Theatre, Ev Lunning, Niccolò Machiavelli, Donald Margulies, Liz Marshall, Leon Pownall, Mario Puzo, Brian Quirt, Angela Rebeiro & Playwrights Canada Press, Virginia Reh & ScriptLab, Marc Richard, Sue "Rider, F. W. Rolfe, Virginia Roncetti & WorkShop Theatre, Lee Sankowich & Marin Theatre Company, Jeffrey Sweet & New York Writers Bloc, ThroughLine, John Van Burek, Bernard Weiner, Scott Wentworth, Alice Wilson & Zachary Scott Theater Center, Michael Wright, and others whose names I have forgotten.

I am especially grateful to the Toronto Fringe Festival, to the talented cast and crew of the first production, and to our enthusiastic audiences.

In addition, I owe much gratitude to Diane Marshall, without whose love and support this play would remain unwritten, while my life would be immeasurably poorer.

Introduction:

Like many plays, *Bella Donna* has been a long time coming. This is especially true in our era of countless readings, workshops, and other noncommittal forms of "producing" plays. In David Copelin's case, his rather full career as a dramaturg in several American theatres preceded his courageous plunge to do for himself what he has always urged for others: to write a work for the stage that tells a compelling story and is delivered with originality and a singular voice. This is no small task, and, as David has learned first-hand, is easier to talk about than to do!

I was very flattered when David came to me and asked me to do some dramaturgical work on *Bella Donna*, which I had heard read in an early draft at Toronto's ScriptLab. We had only recently met, yet he and I quickly became friends. It is interesting and challenging to work dramaturgically with a friend. There was no formal structure of a workshop programme that we could rely upon, as neither of us was then associated with a theatre that did developmental work. For my part, I certainly felt I had my work cut out for me. How should one guide such an accomplished dramaturg in playwriting? Whatever feedback I could give David was no doubt rudimentary, even simplistic. Nevertheless, I soon became aware that the dialogue between us was invaluable to him. Indeed, it wasn't so *much* what I said (David was already cognizant of just about anything I had to contribute); it was that *something* was coming back to him. And herein lies the single most difficult thing for a playwright: *silence*. Not the famous "silences" within a play, *à la* Pinter, or as Michel Tremblay's Madeleine says "...If you've never heard the roar of my silence, Claude, you're not a real writer." No, it is the external, deafening silence that so often follows the inner turmoil of the writing process. I often think there are two kinds of *absolute* silence: one is that of outer space; the other is the one we so frequently encounter once we have sent the fruits of our creative labour out into the wide world. While the first one would kill us instantly were we exposed to it, the second can kill us very, very slowly... unless we have nerves of steel, the patience of Job and profound inner strength.

In any case, I could give David some much-needed attention as we discussed the whys of *Bella Donna*, what he wanted his play to be and how he thought he could get it there.

There was plenty of back-and-forth, often accompanied by rewrites from David, sometimes with no discernible changes as far as I could tell. Still, I remained encouraged and enthusiastic because it was clear that he was genuinely working on his script. This may seem obvious but is not always the case. Often a writer will "seize up" after a couple of drafts and in revising, will either sabotage what made the script interesting in the first place, or simply move a few commas around.

With *Bella Donna*, the most tangible proof of progress was the way in which the number of characters continued to shrink, not for the false reason of economics, but because David saw that he was diffusing the dramatic tension by introducing too many people who existed for too little time on stage. The story could not be played out as well with so many characters. Also, the dialogue grew progressively leaner. David has an excellent ear for clever dialogue, but often, especially in the early drafts, there was too much snap and not enough punch.

It is interesting to see how a writer with verve can use that talent as a brake behind which he or she can conveniently hide, shooting out zippy arrows of dialogue, one-liners, clever puns, that may seem funny at first blush but which frequently take the audience out of the play and the actor out of character. Most of all, they prevent the writer from engaging fully in the story. They contribute to that unpleasant feeling we get when we sense that the playwright insists on poking his head out from behind the curtain to remind the audience that this is all thanks to him. With every new draft, I could see the play moving forward and the writer stepping back. By the time it got to the stage, in the Toronto Fringe Festival, we knew that *the play* was funny and we didn't think of the playwright. This was and is a good thing.

There is every reason to hope that David Copelin will continue to listen to his inner voices and to write down what they say. A new play is working on him. Wait for it.

John Van Burek
Toronto, October 2005

To The Reader:

One night in Paris some years ago I went to see a revival of Victor Hugo's 1833 play *Lucrèce Borgia*. At the time, I only knew that Lucrezia Borgia d'Este (1480-1519) had lived, and was notorious for something or other, and that I was going to see a well-known French actress in the title role. I'd heard some juicy gossip about both women, so I looked forward to the performance as a guilty pleasure, if nothing more. I was happily surprised to find that the drama's energy, wit, bold actions and colourful *tirades* transcended its heavily coincidental plot and sentimental characterizations. The actress made evocative, sensitive choices, and the character she played fascinated me.

Moreover, Hugo's text got past my defences, my Brecht-and-Beckett inspired notions of what a play "should" be, and I have always paid attention to plays that manage that. As a wise woman once told me, when I was lecturing on play genres, "There are only two kinds of plays: those that give you energy, and those that take it away." I believe her.

Who *was* Lucrezia Borgia, anyway? I researched Lucrezia's life and times, inhaling, digesting, asking questions. I became steadily less reverent toward Hugo's text, and toward the historians he relied on; many have blackened Lucrezia's reputation for five centuries. I gave myself permission to adapt the script more assertively, to invent, to create something new. The title changed. Draft followed draft, reading followed reading. Hugo's cast of 27 or so dwindled to 15, then to 10, to 7, finally to 5. The play's "spine" changed. New characters (and new anachronisms—I love 'em) evolved. Now the play is a dark comedy, certainly inspired by Victor Hugo's drama, but very, very different from it. If *Bella Donna* has any truth to it, it's not because I have stuck to provable historical fact. Rather the opposite: I can hold "the mirror up to nature," as Hamlet says we should, but with mirrors and human nature being what they are, there's a lot of room to... *play*.

So, the journey from Paris to Toronto has been long, but it's been one well worth taking, especially with the help I've had along the way. Many people have now seen in *Bella Donna* what I hoped they would see.

May you be among them. May this play give you energy.

David Copelin
Toronto, October 2005

PRODUCTION CREDITS

Some Strange Reason's production of *Bella Donna* opened at the
Factory Studio Theatre in Toronto, Ontario on July 8, 2005.

Cast in order of appearance:

GIOVANNI ....Nick Abraham

ANGELA ....Lindsay McMahon

ALFONSO ....*Stephen Sparks

LUCREZIA ....*Françoise Balthazar

SISTER BIBIANA ....*Mimi Mekler

Director ....*Sue Miner
Set and Costume Designers .... Jackie Chan & Nina Okens
Sound Designers ....Sue Miner & Alexa Carroll
Fight Director ....*Daniel Levinson
Stage Manager ....*Alexa Carroll
Program & Poster Design ....Cathy Elliott

   * Courtesy of Canadian Actors Equity Association

BELLA DONNA

CHARACTERS
in order of appearance:

GIOVANNI
Early twenties. A soldier. Restless, moody, lightning ready to strike.

ANGELA diGhilini
Mid-teens. A countess. Sensual, self-centred, with a lot to learn.

ALFONSO d'Este
Mid-forties. Duke of Ferrara. Robust, devious, decisive.

LUCREZIA Borgia d'Este
Early forties. Duchess of Ferrara. Daughter of Rodrigo Borgia, the late Pope Alexander VI. She is bright, passionate, full of untapped warmth.

Sister BIBIANA
Mid-fifties. A nun of a different order.

Offstage voices include CROWDS, SOLDIERS, GUARDS, and a CAT.

TIME AND PLACE
Rome and Ferrara, Italy, in the early 16th century.

ACT I

Scene 1

    GIOVANNI alone, in the uniform of the Pope's Guard.

GIOVANNI   (*to us*) The new Pope has spoken. Pope Julius II, by God's grace anointed earthly vicar of our blessèd Lord Jesus Christ. Finally a Pope—my Pope—is worthy of the Church! The Borgia Pope is dead, and his whole sordid family is scattered to the winds. They'll get what they deserve—especially Lucrezia, that poisonous... I can see my face in my boot. Soon I'll see her face under it.

    He shows us a red silk scarf, torn in half.

I may not know who I am, but I know what I can do. Holy Father! I, Captain Giovanni, I pledge to win your just war on the Borgia parasites!

    He sings, to the tune of "Santa Lucia":

I'M GOING TO CATCH THE WITCH,
AND THEN I'LL KILL HER DEAD.
I'M GOING TO BASH THE BITCH,
LUCREZIA BORGIA!
I WILL CUT OFF HER HEAD,
BUT FIRST SHE'LL SCRATCH MY ITCH,
AND THEN I'LL KILL THE BITCH,
LUCREZIA BORGIA!

    GIOVANNI flings the scarf into the air, then draws his dagger and catches the scarf on its point. Lights down.

ACT I

Scene 2

> *Ferrara, the Duke's palace. A formal room containing two ornate thrones. One bears the crest of the d'Este family. The other bears the crest of the Borgias. The thrones are placed side by side, equal in power. A bowl of apples sits on a stand.*
>
> *As lights dim up, Countess ANGELA diGhilini enters cautiously. Finding no one, she moves with greater assurance. She chooses an apple, takes one defiant bite, then puts the apple back into the bowl so that the bite does not show. She caresses the d'Este throne, then kicks the Borgia throne and slouches on it disrespectfully. After a moment, ALFONSO d'Este, Duke of Ferrara, strides in and sweeps off his cloak.*

ALFONSO *Contessa.*

ANGELA My lord Duke! You're late.

ALFONSO I'm never late, Angela. The party starts when I arrive.

ANGELA I can't wait. Come and play with me.

ALFONSO What are you doing on my wife's throne?

ANGELA Practicing.

ALFONSO Practicing what?

ANGELA You keep saying I should sit up straight. So—

ALFONSO Angela, don't lie. Look at me.

ANGELA No, Alfonso. You look at me.

> *They look at each other, then meet in a fierce kiss. ALFONSO picks her up and carries her toward his throne.*

ALFONSO Now then, what game shall we play?

ANGELA   Do me.

ALFONSO   Do you? On my throne?

ANGELA   First on your throne. Then on hers.

ALFONSO   God, you're shameless.

ANGELA   You like that.

ALFONSO   Do I?

ANGELA   Yes, you do. You want me.

ALFONSO   How do you know?

ANGELA   Hard evidence. Give it to me.

ALFONSO   Give it to me…?

ANGELA   Give it to me now!

ALFONSO   When you want something, you say…?

ANGELA   Alfonso!

ALFONSO   Manners…

ANGELA   Please.

ALFONSO   I'm sorry. I didn't quite hear…

ANGELA   Please!

ALFONSO   That's better.

> *They go at it. Enter LUCREZIA Borgia d'Este,*
> *Duchess of Ferrara. She is in her 40s. Dusty,*
> *travel-stained, she stops short at what she sees.*
> *She takes an apple from the bowl—it is ANGELA's.*
> *LUCREZIA discovers the bite marks, and that does*
> *it! She puts down the apple, then takes out a dagger*
> *and stabs ALFONSO's throne. ALFONSO jumps*
> *off ANGELA.*

ANGELA   *Donna* Lucrezia!

ALFONSO   So. My wandering wife returns.

LUCREZIA Need a few more seconds?

ALFONSO   Don't start.

LUCREZIA   Sorry to interrupt, but this is more important.

ANGELA   What is?

LUCREZIA   This.

> *She produces a beribboned scroll and shows it to*
> *ALFONSO. ANGELA grabs it and examines the*
> *seal.*

ANGELA   It's from the new Pope!

> *ALFONSO takes the scroll from her.*

ALFONSO   The new Pope. You can put a tiara on a turd, but it
                still smells like shit.

ANGELA   Don't say that! He's the Holy Father!

> *ALFONSO breaks the seal and starts reading.*

ALFONSO   He can't do this.

ANGELA   Do what?

LUCREZIA   He has done it.

> *She takes the scroll from ALFONSO, and reads:*

                "For crimes so loathsome that to name them one
                after another would set this parchment aflame—"

ALFONSO   Melodramatic prick.

LUCREZIA   "—we denounce Duke Alfonso d'Este of Ferrara
                and his infamous spouse *Donna* Lucrezia Borgia as
                atheists, apostates, avatars of anti-Christ! We
                hereby excommunicate them and all their subjects
                from the community of the faithful, and at the wish
                of our sovereign God, we consign them to eternal
                torment in the blackest pit of Hell."

ANGELA   All your subjects?

LUCREZIA   Except priests, nuns, and anyone who betrays us.

ALFONSO   That's quite an incentive.

ANGELA   I'm excommunicated too?

LUCREZIA	I'm afraid so. Committed any mortal sins lately?
ALFONSO	All those cardinals who were so loyal to your father: where are they now?
LUCREZIA	They kiss the ring, not whose finger it's on.
ALFONSO	It's not the ring they kiss.
ANGELA	Alfonso, I don't want to go to hell.
ALFONSO	Nobody's going to hell.
LUCREZIA	Almost nobody.
ANGELA	But we've all been excommunicated.
ALFONSO	By a braggart and a blowhard. We'll soon be back in the bosom of Holy Mother Church.
ANGELA	When?
ALFONSO	I don't know.
LUCREZIA	We need a plan.
ALFONSO	I'm listening.
LUCREZIA	So is someone else.
ALFONSO	Who? Angela? She's old enough.
LUCREZIA	You mean she's young enough.
ALFONSO	Maybe she can help.
LUCREZIA	Maybe she can get out of our throne room and stay out.
ALFONSO	May I remind you that Countess Angela diGhilini is our ward? We owe her protection.
LUCREZIA	But who will protect her from you?
ANGELA	Face it, Lucrezia, he loves me.
LUCREZIA	Oh, child, he'd love a knothole in a wood fence, but God created splinters.
ALFONSO	Lucrezia, help me.
LUCREZIA	You want my help?

ALFONSO   Of course I want your help. What's wrong with you?

ANGELA   Excuse me? I am still here.

LUCREZIA   Why?

ANGELA   Alfonso, the Pope doesn't hate you, he hates her. Beg the Pope for a divorce!

ALFONSO   The Church doesn't permit divorce.

ANGELA   I bet he'd make an exception!

ALFONSO   It's not an option.

ANGELA   She's no use to you any more. Her father's dead.

ALFONSO   That's none of your—

ANGELA   You could kill her. Like she killed her second husband!

LUCREZIA   That's a lie! My brother did that.

ANGELA   Kill her! Since the Church doesn't permit divorce.

ALFONSO   Stop it.

ANGELA   At least think about it.

LUCREZIA   Oh, he does. Now shoo!

ANGELA   Shoo?

LUCREZIA   Yes, dear.

ANGELA   You're letting her kick me out!

ALFONSO   I'll come to you later.

ANGELA   Maybe I'll be busy later.

ALFONSO   Maybe you won't.

ANGELA   Don't you take me for granted.

LUCREZIA   *Arrivederci, cara.*

ANGELA   And you stink of horses. Take a bath.

ANGELA leaves.

LUCREZIA	Your conquests aren't usually so feisty. I like her.
ALFONSO	(*reading the scroll*) Mmmmh. When your father was Pope, I was Captain-General of the Roman Catholic Church. Now I'm the excrement of ten thousand devils.
LUCREZIA	From this Pope, that's a promotion.
ALFONSO	First he'll incite our citizens to rebel against us, then he'll invade Ferrara to "restore civil order." Mouthing pieties as he steals everything he can get his hands on.
LUCREZIA	Sweet revenge on my father. And on me.
ALFONSO	Revenge on a dead man and a woman. Hail the conquering hero! We need to buy time.
LUCREZIA	Yes. Let's write Julius a fawning letter. Beg him to suspend the excommunication in exchange for... a significant increase in our annual tribute to the Holy See.
ALFONSO	How significant?
LUCREZIA	Enough to get his attention. He may order us to come to Rome.
ALFONSO	I don't think we'll go. Offer him...
LUCREZIA	Double Ferrara's usual tribute.
ALFONSO	Double?
LUCREZIA	We tell him that we fear his power. It's no lie. Then... then we plead with him to send some high official here to receive our utterly abject submission to his spiritual and temporal majesty.
ALFONSO	Utterly abject submission. Yes.
LUCREZIA	The person he sends: better our choice than his.
ALFONSO	Certainly. And no one lower than a cardinal.
LUCREZIA	Agreed. Someone slow.
ALFONSO	Slow and stupid.
LUCREZIA	Slow, and stupid, and long-winded.

They ponder.

ALFONSO &
LUCREZIA   (*together*) Cardinal Vincenzo.

ALFONSO   (*laughing*) Perfect. In the meantime, I'll order more artillery from the Austrian foundries.

LUCREZIA   With what money?

ALFONSO   Our credit's good.

LUCREZIA   It was.

ALFONSO   So we'll raise taxes.

LUCREZIA   Raise taxes? Now?

ALFONSO   For when Julius invades us. Then after we've chased the big pig back to his holy sty, we'll lower the taxes. A little. Reward the people for their loyalty.

LUCREZIA   If we win. And there's no guarantee of that. We've been excommunicated. Denied the sacraments, condemned to everlasting hellfire if we die before the excommunication is lifted. The Pope has the power to loose and to bind. Julius may be a pig, but he's God's pig now.

ALFONSO   Well, well. Lucrezia Borgia—scared.

LUCREZIA   Aren't you?

ALFONSO   Yes. But I'm not going to hell without a fight. Julius really does hate you.

LUCREZIA   He hates you, too. No matter what your little friend says.

ALFONSO   Because I married you. I know. Well. Write him a letter that's truly, um…

LUCREZIA   Obsequious.

ALFONSO   Grovelling. On our knees in the snow of the Alpine passes.

LUCREZIA   Abject self-abasement.

ALFONSO   And make it sincere.

LUCREZIA   I wonder if that's the most effective way to—

ALFONSO   Do you have a better idea?

LUCREZIA   I'm not sure.

ALFONSO   Well then, work on the letter until you do.

LUCREZIA   Alfonso… we used to be so close…

ALFONSO   I still am close. Just not with you. Show me the draft when you're finished. You know where to find me.

ALFONSO exits.

LUCREZIA   Lorenzo!

GUARD   (*off*) *Madonna?*

LUCREZIA   Find Sister Bibiana, and bring her to me. *Subito!*

Lights down.

ACT I

Scene 3

Lights up on a garden in the Vatican. A stone bench. Sister BIBIANA, a nun in her fifties, is reading her breviary. After a moment, a woman, exquisitely dressed and wearing a mask, enters and sits next to BIBIANA. It's GIOVANNI in drag. BIBIANA rises.

BIBIANA   Please excuse me, *madonna.* I don't mean to intrude.

BIBIANA starts to leave.

GIOVANNI   No, Sister. I am the intruder. You were here first.

BIBIANA   *Madonna.* Your voice… it's…

GIOVANNI   Deep?

BIBIANA Deep. You sound… forgive me… like a man.

GIOVANNI A young, handsome man?

BIBIANA I know that voice…

GIOVANNI A young, handsome, witty, virile man?

BIBIANA Captain Giovanni!

GIOVANNI Sister Bibiana!

He removes his mask.

BIBIANA What in the world…?

GIOVANNI Fooled you, didn't I?

BIBIANA Congratulations. I have seen many things, but never before have I seen a captain in the Holy Father's private guard dressed as a woman!

GIOVANNI His Holiness's invitation said, "Costume yourselves as your favourite animal." I obey.

BIBIANA This may be news to a soldier, but women are not animals.

GIOVANNI Not just any woman. Her.

BIBIANA Who?

GIOVANNI La Borgia. You've seen her. Don't I look like her?

BIBIANA Yes, and that's why Pope Julius will be furious.

GIOVANNI He'll love it.

BIBIANA Don't be so sure.

GIOVANNI He loves me. I saved his nephew's life at the siege of Ravenna. I make the old man laugh.

BIBIANA Not about her.

GIOVANNI Besides, he needs me to conquer Ferrara.

BIBIANA Your regiment can conquer Ferrara. You can rot in a dungeon.

GIOVANNI There I'll be at the judging of the costumes, surrounded by tigers and monkeys and butterflies, the only one looking like a human being. The Pope will say, "You're no animal!" And I'll say, "Holiness, I am the nastiest animal in Italy, *Donna* Lucrezia Borgia, here to submit myself to the mercy of the Supreme Pontiff and Holy Church." Then I'll take off my mask. And he'll cackle and clap his hands and toss me a pouch full of gold. Then I'll tell him you said he has no sense of humour. We'll see who rots!

BIBIANA   I'll be there, too. I'll watch that scarlet flush crawl up his neck until he looks like a constipated eggplant. I'll watch when he orders you flayed alive. I'll watch when they slowly separate your skin from your flesh with red hot pincers. You won't die right away. You'll be screaming in agony. I hate that.

GIOVANNI   Never happen.

BIBIANA   Or worse! Say you're right. Say he loves your wit and your courage and he laughs, a big, booming guffaw. He laughs, and then he clutches his heart, he staggers, he falls down the holy stairs, babump, babump, babump, and when they roll him over he's—

GIOVANNI   Bite your tongue!

BIBIANA   And who just killed the Pope? You! Who just ruined the masquerade ball? You! People will have to go home sober. The whispers. The innuendo. "Maybe he's in league with them. Maybe he's one of them!"

GIOVANNI   One of who?

BIBIANA   The Borgias!

GIOVANNI   But I hate the Borgias.

BIBIANA   So what? There you'll be, wearing the dress that killed the Pope, the Borgias' worst enemy. Your patron. The man who took you in, invented you, molded you. Dead. It could happen.

GIOVANNI   Maybe I'd better find another costume.

BIBIANA   Maybe.

> *GIOVANNI leaves. BIBIANA settles herself on the bench and takes out her rosary beads. From another direction, GIOVANNI re-enters, dressed as before. Only it's not GIOVANNI; it's LUCREZIA, dressed and masked exactly as GIOVANNI was.*

What now? Stop wasting time! Go find something less dangerous. No argument. March!

LUCREZIA   Sister Bibiana?

BIBIANA   The voice! Even the voice. You're good at this, but please, don't tempt fate.

LUCREZIA   I have to.

BIBIANA   You've never seen her or heard her speak. How?—

> *LUCREZIA takes off her mask.*

LUCREZIA   What are you babbling about?

BIBIANA   *Madonna!* What are you doing here? If Julius finds out…! You said you'd wait in Ferrara until I got in touch.

LUCREZIA   I'm sick of waiting. And then, the rumours. Tales of a costume ball, a great masquerade, celebrating Giuliano della Rovere's election as Pope Julius II.

BIBIANA   And for that, you risk your life? To go to a party?

LUCREZIA   To see the Pope.

BIBIANA   With respect, *Donna* Lucrezia, you're insane.

LUCREZIA   It's a gamble, Bibiana. If I can get to him alone, in private, I can talk to him. When I was a girl, he was fond of me.

BIBIANA   He was fond of you until you were nineteen.

LUCREZIA   When my father went on manoeuvres and left me in charge of the Vatican.

BIBIANA   Yes, and Julius had expected that honour. He took your appointment as a deliberate slap in the face, which it was.

LUCREZIA   Why? My father made my brother Cesare
            a cardinal when he was twelve.

BIBIANA   Yes, but your brother was never much of
            a cardinal. He kept murdering people. But you ran
            the Vatican pretty well. That's what Julius can't
            forgive. The first thing he did as Pope was to seal
            up your father's apartments. Everything in there
            that was Borgia has vanished. It's as if you never
            existed.

LUCREZIA   I need to see him!

BIBIANA   I've seen him for you, and I've made some
            progress.

LUCREZIA   When will he lift the excommunication?

BIBIANA   Not so fast. He's agreed to send Cardinal Vincenzo
            to Ferrara to "negotiate." That's all.

LUCREZIA   That's something. The people of Ferrara fear their
            prospects in the next world. And so do I.

BIBIANA   Your prospects in this world may not be much.
            Vincenzo's escort will be a full regiment of soldiers.
            You can expect a demand for triple the annual
            tribute.

LUCREZIA   Triple! Alfonso will love that.

BIBIANA   By the way, the Pope asked me where you were.
            I said, "Holiness, *Donna* Lucrezia is in the hands of
            God, as are we all." Then I took my leave.

LUCREZIA   I assume he had you followed.

BIBIANA   Of course. By two rather incompetent thugs.

LUCREZIA   What happened?

            BIBIANA touches the large crucifix she wears.
            Suddenly, a stiletto blade slides out and clicks
            ominously into place.

BIBIANA   I sent their souls to Saint Peter.

LUCREZIA   I hope they're happy wherever they are.

BIBIANA	Amen. There's something else. This masquerade business... when I saw you, I thought... well, one of the Pope's soldiers has a little too much imagination for his own good. My advice to you is to get out of Rome now. I mean it. It's too dangerous for you, and for me.
LUCREZIA	Shhh! Someone's coming.

LUCREZIA replaces her mask.

BIBIANA	*Madonna*, this is important, there's—
LUCREZIA	We mustn't be seen together.
BIBIANA	I'll go. Just keep that mask on!

SISTER BIBIANA leaves. LUCREZIA watches her go. From another direction, GIOVANNI enters. He is still dressed and masked exactly as LUCREZIA is.

GIOVANNI	Sister, I just had a thought...

GIOVANNI sees LUCREZIA and stops dead in his tracks. LUCREZIA turns. GIOVANNI and LUCREZIA stare at each other.

LUCREZIA	Someone's going to pay for this.
GIOVANNI	That dressmaker's dead meat.
LUCREZIA	Ah. A man dressed as a woman. Of course, men in dresses are commonplace here. But what will His Holiness say when he sees you?
GIOVANNI	He'll say, "Bravo!"... I hope.
LUCREZIA	For your sake, I hope so too. But are you me, or am I you?
GIOVANNI	I'm... pardon me, *madonna*, I.... Where's your costume?
LUCREZIA	Excuse me?
GIOVANNI	Your costume. The Pope asked everybody to dress up as their favourite animal.

LUCREZIA   You didn't.

GIOVANNI   Yes, I did.

LUCREZIA   I'm your favourite animal?

GIOVANNI   You? No. How could you be? I don't know who you are.

LUCREZIA   No.

GIOVANNI   I'm dressed as Lucrezia Borgia.

LUCREZIA   Oh, my. Isn't that dangerous?

GIOVANNI   I laugh at danger! I predict the Pope will admire my nerve.

LUCREZIA   I certainly do.

GIOVANNI   Well, sure. You had the same idea. Who are you?

LUCREZIA   A woman wearing a mask.

GIOVANNI   Oh, I see. You're here *incognita*. But what shall I call you?

LUCREZIA   How about *Donna* Lucrezia Borgia? And I'll call you the same.

GIOVANNI   That has possibilities. They say the witch can be in two places at once.

LUCREZIA   Really?

GIOVANNI   Really. But if she were here, she'd scratch your eyes out.

LUCREZIA   Ouch. And what would she do to you?

GIOVANNI   Wrong question. It's what I'd do to her. Thank God the Pope's excommunicated her. We're going to invade Ferrara, and when we do, I'm going to catch that slut and pay her back for every vile thing she and her family have done to Italy.

LUCREZIA   You'll have to stand in line.

GIOVANNI   That line begins behind me.

LUCREZIA   It's a long line, too.

GIOVANNI	That's because the Borgias pray to Satan.
LUCREZIA	Now where did you hear that?
GIOVANNI	It's all over town. They had a black mass right in the Vatican. Lucrezia herself was the priest. Can you imagine a greater blasphemy? And the wine in the chalice wasn't wine. It was...
LUCREZIA	Yes?
GIOVANNI	Well, every month, for a few days, women are... um...
LUCREZIA	Are you trying to say that the chalice was full of Lucrezia's menstrual blood?

> *GIOVANNI retches.*

Who told you this sordid tale? He or she was there and saw it?

GIOVANNI	Almost.
LUCREZIA	Almost. But not quite.
GIOVANNI	Everyone was talking about it.
LUCREZIA	*Vox populi, vox Dei.* Even stupid rumours and lies.
GIOVANNI	I believe in things unseen! I have sworn to punish those horrible, sacrilegious Borgias. I shall take revenge on behalf of the Orsini, the Colonna, the d'Appiani, and all the noble families!
LUCREZIA	In that dress?
GIOVANNI	Huh? No. In my uniform. But first, I'm going to show the Pope... Oh, I just got a great idea! Let's go in together! Both of us! We're going to show the Pope something he's never seen before!
LUCREZIA	I don't think so.
GIOVANNI	Don't worry, I know him personally. We'll announce ourselves as two sides of Lucrezia Borgia's soul.
LUCREZIA	Her soul? You think she has a soul?

GIOVANNI Absolutely. Even Satan was an angel once. So I figure Lucrezia Borgia must have a soul. Probably a pitiful, dried-up little thing by now, but in God's eyes, a soul's a soul. No matter how depraved she is, her soul can be saved. We tell the Pope that we're costumed as a unique animal, a soul in torment, a soul divided between hell and heaven. Then... then we beg him to heal us!

LUCREZIA By making us one soul?

GIOVANNI Exactly! Separate, we're just two victims of a dishonest dressmaker. Together, we're a vision of why the Church exists.

LUCREZIA All right.

GIOVANNI You'll do it?

LUCREZIA You interest me.

GIOVANNI Oh, the love of God excites me. I feel such... such desire!

LUCREZIA Desire? Now?

GIOVANNI Desire always.

LUCREZIA For what?

GIOVANNI For you.

LUCREZIA For me! You haven't even seen my face.

GIOVANNI But behind your mask, I can see your eyes, and they are enough. I desire you. In the country, in the city, in the Vatican, in heaven, even in hell. And you, *madonna* with a secret name: do you feel desire?

LUCREZIA You're very young.

GIOVANNI And you are springtime eternal. You are—

LUCREZIA Stop. I'm older than you are. I have known desire. Are you asking me if I desire to know it again?

GIOVANNI Are you married?

LUCREZIA Sometimes. You?

GIOVANNI No. What do you mean, sometimes?

LUCREZIA Tell me your name.

GIOVANNI Call me Giovanni. Tell me your name.

LUCREZIA Call me Lucrezia.

GIOVANNI As you wish. A gentleman does not pry.

LUCREZIA Look up, Giovanni. What do you see?

GIOVANNI Stars.

LUCREZIA They're watching us.

GIOVANNI They're watching over us.

LUCREZIA A beautiful night.

GIOVANNI It is.

LUCREZIA We're alone here.

GIOVANNI We are.

LUCREZIA I wonder.

GIOVANNI About what?

LUCREZIA About you.

GIOVANNI You don't have to wonder. You can know.

  GIOVANNI removes his mask.

LUCREZIA Here I am.

  LUCREZIA removes her mask.

GIOVANNI *Madonna.* You are beautiful.

LUCREZIA So are you.

  As if inventing a ritual, they exchange masks.

GIOVANNI Come. First to the Pope.

LUCREZIA Yes. And then.

GIOVANNI And then.

GIOVANNI and LUCREZIA put each other's masks on, then run off. ALFONSO, dressed as a lion, bursts from the shadows. Furious, stiletto in hand, he starts offstage. ANGELA, dressed as a lamb, scurries after him and grabs his arm.

ALFONSO   Damn you, Angela!

ANGELA   Let them go.

ALFONSO   Get out of my way!

ANGELA   Why? So you can kill her in front of the Pope while you're excommunicated? Lose your life, lose your soul, lose Ferrara? For her?

ALFONSO   (*in torment*) Lucrezia!

ANGELA   Forget Lucrezia. Remember me.

ALFONSO   Go away.

ANGELA   Let me hold you.

ALFONSO   Don't touch me!

ANGELA   If that's what you want. But I'm here.

ALFONSO   (*to the absent LUCREZIA*) I can wait. Until I get you back in Ferrara.

He leaves the stage.

ANGELA   (*to herself*) You can pretend I don't exist except when you want me. But I do exist. I do.

Lights down.

ACT I

Scene 4

Lights up on a huge bed. LUCREZIA and GIOVANNI have just finished making love.

LUCREZIA   I'm impressed.

GIOVANNI   I'm hungry.

LUCREZIA   Me too. Yumyumyum.

> *She nibbles on him.*

GIOVANNI   What am I, a piece of meat?

LUCREZIA   Filet mignon.

GIOVANNI   No. Filet mignon is boneless.

> *LUCREZIA laughs.*

LUCREZIA   Nice talk.

GIOVANNI   Nice night.

LUCREZIA   Yes.

GIOVANNI   Two halves of a lost soul, reunited.

LUCREZIA   When you told him what animal we were, he glared at us so hard, I thought he was going to explode. Then he laughed! And blessed us! It's a miracle.

> *GIOVANNI pulls the moneybag from the clothing next to the bed.*

GIOVANNI   And I'm a prophet!

LUCREZIA   I can't believe we got away with it. I was terrified.

GIOVANNI   You were spectacular.

LUCREZIA   I was?

GIOVANNI   Amazing.

LUCREZIA   Then I ran away.

GIOVANNI   Then we ran away. Together.

LUCREZIA   And here we are.

GIOVANNI   Which is where, I wonder?

LUCREZIA   The Borgia apartments.

GIOVANNI   What? I thought Pope Julius had them sealed up.

LUCREZIA   He did.

GIOVANNI   Then how... a secret entrance?

LUCREZIA   There used to be four. There's one that stayed a secret.

GIOVANNI   You've been here before.

LUCREZIA   Once or twice.

GIOVANNI   One of the old Pope's mistresses, eh?

LUCREZIA   Some people thought so.

GIOVANNI   Well. He's dead. And your taste has improved.

LUCREZIA   Flatter yourself!

GIOVANNI   The lair of Rodrigo Borgia. It's creepy.

LUCREZIA   He used to sleep in this bed.

GIOVANNI   (*crossing himself*) God! We made love in it.

LUCREZIA   Really, Giovanni. It's just a bed.

GIOVANNI   No bed with you in it is "just a bed."

> *Delighted by this, LUCREZIA looks at GIOVANNI, then kisses him deeply. Slowly, GIOVANNI takes her foot from under the covers and begins to lick and kiss her toes. LUCREZIA abandons herself to sensation. After a moment, Sister BIBIANA enters cautiously. She sees the lovers and watches for a moment. Then:*

BIBIANA   Stop that. Get up, both of you.

LUCREZIA   Bibiana!

BIBIANA   *Donna* Lucrezia.

GIOVANNI   *Donna* Lucrezia? Lucrezia who?

BIBIANA   No time for chitchat. Put these on. Now.

> *BIBIANA throws a nun's habit to LUCREZIA and a soldier's uniform and boots to GIOVANNI. During the following, they dress.*

GIOVANNI	Sister, I'm naked here. Turn away.
BIBIANA	Don't be stupid. The halls are swarming with soldiers. They're searching for you on the Pope's orders. If I can find you, they can find you.
GIOVANNI	So what? I'm a soldier.
BIBIANA	You're an idiot. Now put your feet in your boots and get out.
LUCREZIA	Bibiana, I told him who I am. But he didn't believe me.
BIBIANA	What?
GIOVANNI	She told me to call her Lucrezia Borgia. But that's absurd. She can't be. She's. You mean, I. We. No. No. Oh, my God!
BIBIANA	Suffer somewhere else. Let's go!
GIOVANNI	Wait! *Donna* Lucrezia Borgia, you are under arrest!

The two women stare at him, then burst out laughing.

BIBIANA	Right, then. Drag her to the Pope. Go ahead. I can't wait to hear what the angriest, most impatient and most hung-over man in Italy will say when he learns where, how, and with whom you spent the night.

Beat.

GIOVANNI	Jesus Christ.
BIBIANA	Amen.
GIOVANNI	(*to BIBIANA*) I thought you were my friend. You're her spy. Traitor!
BIBIANA	I didn't have to bring that uniform, you know. Show a little gratitude.

From offstage, we hear the sounds of a search party.

We have to go.

GIOVANNI   (*to LUCREZIA*) Borgia! I kissed your foul mouth. God knows where it's been and what's been in it.

LUCREZIA   I have nothing to be ashamed of. Do you?

GIOVANNI   You fucked your own brother. You fucked your own father.

BIBIANA   Worse. She fucked you.—Here. You earned it.

BIBIANA tosses the pouch full of gold to GIOVANNI. He catches it, then drops it scornfully and spits at LUCREZIA.

LUCREZIA   Goodbye, Giovanni.

LUCREZIA and BIBIANA leave. Offstage, the search party gets closer. GIOVANNI picks up the pouch and hides it in his uniform.

GIOVANNI   In here! I found their costumes! They can't be far away!

Lights down.

ACT I

Scene 5

GIOVANNI, to us, in a spotlight.

GIOVANNI   I gargle with cheap brandy. I scrape my tongue until it bleeds. I scrub my cock with a wire brush. I still feel dirty. Nightmares. She rapes me. Milks me dry. God! I wake up moaning, sweating stuck to the sheets. Lucrezia Borgia. Princess of poison, sorceress of sex, stilettos and strangulation. How could I...? But she... she touched me. Caressed me. Melted me into a million stars. O God, I want her again, I know who she is and what she is and I still want her, no, that's the devil talking, get thee behind me, Satan...!

Lights dim up on a public square in Ferrara, just outside the palace.

Calm down, for God's sake, control yourself, Giovanni, you're in uniform, in public, right in front of her palace! Her palace...

Upstage, there's an arch that reads B O R G I A in metal letters.

Citizens of Ferrara! Look upon the lair of incest, adultery, witchcraft, murder, hypocrisy, treason, and lust!

Inflamed with self-righteousness, GIOVANNI climbs the arch. Using his dagger, he pries off the letters B and A and drops them onto the stage. The arch now reads: O R G I. The offstage CROWD responds with laughter, indignant comments, and ribald jests. Realizing what he's done, GIOVANNI runs off. Enter BIBIANA from another direction.

BIBIANA   Go home! Pray for your immortal souls. There's nothing to see here. (*to us:*) That boy is handy with a dagger, but brains? He's a little impulsive. I have to tell Lucrezia and Alfonso. But whom shall I tell first? As always, God will guide me.

BIBIANA takes a coin from her pocket, flips it, and looks at it.

The Lord has spoken. Blessèd be the name of the Lord.

She exits into the palace.
Lights down.

ACT I

Scene 6

Ferrara. Lights up on the throne room. A table with a crystal tray, bearing a gold flagon, a silver flagon and elegant enamel cups. ALFONSO is reading documents.

LUCREZIA (*off*) Alfonso! Alfonso!

LUCREZIA rushes in.

Alfonso! Someone just vandalized my name on the palace gate. In broad daylight.

ALFONSO Vandalized your name? How so?

LUCREZIA Go see for yourself. Stand among your sweaty subjects, look at the Borgia arch, and listen to them snicker.

ALFONSO Thank you, no.

LUCREZIA It's treason!

ALFONSO Come, sweetheart, sit down. We'll have some wine, and—

LUCREZIA I don't want wine. I want justice.

ALFONSO Justice! We're excommunicated. It might be wiser to ask for mercy.

LUCREZIA Don't patronize me.

ALFONSO Lucrezia, that's good Christian doctrine.

LUCREZIA Stay inert, then. I'll find the guilty swine myself and give him what he deserves.

ALFONSO Calm down.

LUCREZIA No! You get angry!

ALFONSO I don't have time for anger.

LUCREZIA Make time. Or are you afraid he might be a better swordsman?

ALFONSO Anything's possible.

LUCREZIA Find that man! Arrest him!

ALFONSO Lucrezia, I did. And I did.

LUCREZIA You devil. You're way ahead of me.

ALFONSO   This time.

LUCREZIA   Who is this person?

ALFONSO   Nobody I know.

LUCREZIA   Where is he?

ALFONSO   Next door. I'm about to interrogate him.

LUCREZIA   Alfonso, swear to me that the man will not leave here alive.

ALFONSO   If that's what you want.

LUCREZIA   Swear!

ALFONSO   Lucrezia, you have my word of honour. He dies today.—Bring the prisoner in!

> *GIOVANNI is pushed in, roughly, by unseen hands. Still in uniform, he is manacled, and his feet are chained. He has been badly beaten. LUCREZIA reacts, then controls herself.*

ALFONSO   (*to GIOVANNI*) Come here. Who are you?

GIOVANNI   My lord Duke: my name is Giovanni.

ALFONSO   Giovanni what?

GIOVANNI   Just Giovanni. I don't know my family name. I am a captain in the personal guard of Pope Julius.

ALFONSO   You serve in the most elite unit in Italy, yet you don't know your name or family?

GIOVANNI   No, your grace. I assume I'm illegitimate.

ALFONSO   There are no illegitimate children, only illegitimate parents. And they are more common than you might think. Even our belovèd spouse *Donna* Lucrezia Borgia d'Este, here beside us, was a… love child. Did you know that?

GIOVANNI   All Europe knows it, your grace.—No offence meant, *madonna*.

ALFONSO   And none taken, I'm sure.

LUCREZIA   (*bitterly*) Get on with it.

ALFONSO How did you manage to get into the Pope's guard without a pedigree?

GIOVANNI I made my own pedigree. The Holy Father knows a warrior when he sees one.

ALFONSO That he does. Tell us more.

GIOVANNI Five years ago, I was a fisherman, the only child of Stefano and Anna Rossi. We had to fish every day just to survive. There was a big storm. Our boat capsized. Stefano and Anna couldn't swim. I tried to save them…. Their bodies washed up on the beach. After the funeral, Father Giuseppe told me that Stefano and Anna Rossi weren't my parents. I wasn't Giovanni Rossi. There was no Giovanni Rossi. I was just a nameless baby in a basket abandoned at the church door. So I left my village. I learned to read. I learned to fight. I learned the world.

ALFONSO With no clue at all to your identity?

GIOVANNI None. Well, one.

ALFONSO Go on.

GIOVANNI When they found me, I was wrapped in half a red silk scarf. But it hasn't helped me find my parents.

ALFONSO What a pity. Well. To business. Captain, this morning, a person or persons unknown defaced the Borgia arch in the public square. Do you know anything about this crime?

GIOVANNI Yes, your grace, I do.

ALFONSO What do you know?

GIOVANNI I committed it.

ALFONSO I see. I won't ask why you did so. Given your rather disconcerting candour, I fear that you would tell me.

GIOVANNI *Don* Alfonso, I expressly waive any rights that I may have under Cardinal Vincenzo's diplomatic immunity. *Donna* Lucrezia, I am sorry for what

I did. It was dishonourable. I accept whatever punishment you decide is appropriate.

ALFONSO Punishment. Well. As for that—

LUCREZIA *Don* Alfonso, I must speak with you. In private.

ALFONSO Certainly, my love—Captain, would you please excuse us for a moment?

> *GIOVANNI bows and shuffles out.*

LUCREZIA Alfonso—

ALFONSO Nice lad. I almost hate to kill him.

LUCREZIA No—

ALFONSO But I gave you my word, so that's that.

LUCREZIA Alfonso, don't kill that boy.

ALFONSO Beg pardon?

LUCREZIA I don't want him to die.

ALFONSO I gave you my word of honour.

LUCREZIA If I'm willing to pardon this Giovanni—is that his name?—what difference does it make to you? I'm the one he offended.

ALFONSO Just so. He offended you. That is unpardonable.

LUCREZIA If we seek mercy rather than justice, we should grant it, too.

ALFONSO Dear Lucrezia.

LUCREZIA Executing a puny little Vatican mercenary? What would we gain?

ALFONSO The lion and his lioness don't get upset over a fleabite.

LUCREZIA Exactly! Thank you, Alfonso.

ALFONSO Thank me after his funeral.

LUCREZIA His—

ALFONSO I have given my word. Captain Giovanni must die.

LUCREZIA	Spare his life. Just until Cardinal Vincenzo leaves for Rome. Then I'll take care of him myself.
ALFONSO	I can't do it.
LUCREZIA	Of course you can!
ALFONSO	I won't do it.
LUCREZIA	Whyever not?
ALFONSO	Because Giovanni No Name is your lover.
	Beat.
LUCREZIA	That's ridiculous. He just defaced my name in public.
ALFONSO	Lovers quarrel.
LUCREZIA	Oh, Alfonso, they've even got you believing the lies. That hurts.
ALFONSO	Come off it, Lucrezia. I was there. I saw you panting after him like a bitch in heat. I watched you exchange masks and drag him into the Vatican, and I've had enough of this shame and disgrace and betrayal!
LUCREZIA	You hypocrite! Have you also had enough of that insect Angela?
ALFONSO	That's different.
LUCREZIA	How?
ALFONSO	I'm a man.
LUCREZIA	In some ways.
ALFONSO	In all ways. Maybe you've forgotten.
LUCREZIA	Alfonso... "for better and for worse." I said that the day we were married. I meant it, then and now.
ALFONSO	Sure you do. Without me, your throat would be cut in a minute.
LUCREZIA	Without me, your throat would have been cut years ago.

ALFONSO   Speculation.

LUCREZIA   When you married me, you got a fortune for
a dowry, the cities of Spoleto and Rimini to pay
you tribute, an alliance with Rome and the
protection of the Borgia family. I made you the
most powerful duke in Europe.

ALFONSO   And I made you respectable. At least I tried.

LUCREZIA   Well, aren't you the martyr! But look at you now.
Bankrupt. Excommunicated. Facing an invasion
and civil war. Denying the facts by milking your
adolescent cow. My father's dead, and yet you still
don't have the guts to throw me to the wolves.
Why not? Go ahead! Pawn my jewellery, buy more
cannon, invade Rome, depose the Pope, rule the
world! While Angela rules you.

ALFONSO   You Borgias. Your bloodthirsty brother Cesare, with
his face turned into Swiss cheese by syphilis. Your
other brothers, connivers with the combined brains
of a retarded rat. Your mother Vannozza, the
Vatican whore, littering Rome with her nasty
bastards while she sucked and fucked her way into
a fortune in real estate. And last but not least, your
father Rodrigo, Pope Alexander VI, the Pope with
a harem! Condemning honest men to prison and
turning the College of Cardinals into a joke. So
rotten inside when he died that he blew up like
a pig's bladder on a stick. And the stink! It was
his putrid soul, on its way to hell.

LUCREZIA   I loved my father!

ALFONSO   So I've heard. Now listen: I want Giovanni to die.
But let's be fair. You may choose the way he dies.—
Cat got your tongue? Pity. I'll just tell the guard to
cut his throat.

LUCREZIA   Stop!

ALFONSO   Or you can pour him a refreshing cup of wine.

LUCREZIA   Alfonso, that's what I planned to do all along. Only
in my own good time, when he's least expecting it.

ALFONSO   Right this minute suits me better. Give me your
          hand. Yes, here's the famous ring. Lift up the stone,
          and—Look! It's full of some exotic powder. We'll
          just open the gold flagon, like so, and pour in that
          good old Borgia magic.—A little shake. All done.—
          Outside there! Send in the prisoner!

          GIOVANNI returns.

          Captain Giovanni, hear your fate: *Donna* Lucrezia
          pardons you. Therefore, I pardon you. God forbid
          that we should deprive the Church of a faithful
          sword in a faithful hand.

          *ALFONSO unshackles GIOVANNI and returns his
          dagger.*

GIOVANNI Clemency? I didn't expect this. I—

ALFONSO   We're not such monsters. Are we, dearest? Tell us,
          what exactly are your duties in Rome?

GIOVANNI I command a company of fifty lancers.

ALFONSO   Lancers! Excellent. May I ask you a personal
          question?

GIOVANNI I would be honoured.

ALFONSO   What sort of salary does the Pope pay you?

GIOVANNI The Holy Father gives me two thousand ducats
          a year. Out of that, I pay, feed and clothe my men
          and myself. Bonuses and battlefield souvenirs are
          extra.

ALFONSO   Of course. Now: suppose we offer you five
          thousand ducats a year.

GIOVANNI Five thousand!

ALFONSO   Will you join our service?

GIOVANNI I'm sorry, your grace, but…

ALFONSO   Once this annoying excommunication is lifted, of
          course.

GIOVANNI   That's not it. I have given my word of honour to
            serve the Holy Father for the next three years.
            I may not break a sacred oath.

ALFONSO   A man whose word of honour means something!
            I like that. May we offer you some wine?

GIOVANNI   *Don* Alfonso, this morning I disgraced my uniform.
            This afternoon, from you and *Donna* Lucrezia, I am
            learning what Christian forgiveness is. I will gladly
            drink with you.

ALFONSO   Splendid.

            *ALFONSO pours a drink from the silver flagon
            into an enamel cup. He hands another cup to
            LUCREZIA.*

            Donna Lucrezia, to show our respect for this loyal
            servant of the Supreme Pontiff, will you please
            pour?

            LUCREZIA tries to take the silver flagon.

            No, dear. Only the best of wine for the best of men.

            *Shaking, LUCREZIA pours GIOVANNI a cup of
            wine from the gold flagon.*

GIOVANNI   You do me honour. I thank you both.

ALFONSO   Our pleasure. May you be in love until the moment
            you die.

GIOVANNI   *Don* Alfonso, that's the best toast I've ever heard.
            The same to you and… and *Donna* Lucrezia.

            *GIOVANNI and ALFONSO touch cups and sip
            with ritualistic delicacy.*

            This wine is fantastic!

ALFONSO   It's a very special vintage. Captain, I regret I cannot
            stay and chat. Affairs of state. You understand.

GIOVANNI   I hope that you and the Holy Father can resolve
            your differences.

ALFONSO   I'm an optimist. Farewell, Captain.

GIOVANNI   Your grace.

ALFONSO   (*to LUCREZIA*) Stay with him. Share your lover's last few moments of life. You might even have time for a final tryst. If you skip the foreplay.

ALFONSO leaves.

GIOVANNI   *Donna* Lucrezia, I—

LUCREZIA   Giovanni! You just drank poison!

GIOVANNI   Poison? God, I should have suspected. Lucrezia Borgia poured the wine!

LUCREZIA   Alfonso knows we were lovers. He gave me a choice: watch a guard cut your throat, or give you—

GIOVANNI   Poison. And you chose.

LUCREZIA   If your throat's cut, you die. But there's an antidote to the Borgia poison! I'm the only one who knows that it exists. Here.

She tries to put a vial to GIOVANNI's lips. He recoils.

GIOVANNI   Not so fast! How do I know that *that* isn't poison?

LUCREZIA   Giovanni, I'm trying to save your life!

GIOVANNI   Why?

LUCREZIA   Because—There's no time to argue. Drink!

GIOVANNI   No! The Duke is an honourable man. You are… well, we both know what you are. In Rome I insulted you. Here in Ferrara I've turned your name into a public joke.

LUCREZIA   Do you want to die? Soon even the antidote won't save you. Drink it now! Drink it now!

Beat.

GIOVANNI   You drink it.

LUCREZIA   What?—Yes!

GIOVANNI   First the poisoned wine. Lots of it!

> *LUCREZIA drinks greedily from the gold flagon.*

Now this so-called antidote.

> *LUCREZIA sucks from the vial. They wait in silence for awhile.*

LUCREZIA Giovanni—

GIOVANNI Another minute.

LUCREZIA For the love of God!

GIOVANNI What do you care whether I live or die?

LUCREZIA Giovanni, I am Lucrezia Borgia. Am I the woman you thought Lucrezia Borgia was?

GIOVANNI No. But I—

LUCREZIA Then take the antidote. Right now. Giovanni, I beg you. Don't wait any longer. Please!

> *She looks into his eyes. Mesmerized, he drinks from the vial.*

LUCREZIA Saved!—Keep that vial with you always. You might need it again some day. Now get out of this palace as fast as you can.

GIOVANNI How?

LUCREZIA Take this passageway. Leave Ferrara, and please, for your sake, and for mine, don't ever come back.

> *GIOVANNI hesitates, then kisses LUCREZIA with a passion that shakes them both. He leaves. Exhausted, LUCREZIA sinks onto a throne. Lights down.*

ACT I

Scene 7

> *Ferrara. ANGELA's bedchamber. A curtained bed. The curtains are wide open, and ANGELA is sitting*

> *cross-legged on the bed. She has two hand puppets.*
> *She begins to play with the puppets, which*
> *represent Pope Alexander VI and Pope Julius II.*

ANGELA   (*as Julius*) I'm the Pope.

(*as Alexander*) No, I'm the Pope.

(*as Julius*) You were the Pope.

(*as Alexander*) I am Rodrigo Borgia! The whole world knows me and loves me and honours me as Pope Alexander the Sixth.

(*as Julius*) Feel that fire? Smell that brimstone?

(*as Alexander*) You farted?

(*as Julius*) You're dead. You're in hell.

(*as Alexander*) Is that so. And just who in hell are you?

(*as Julius*) I am your old rival Giuliano della Rovere. Now the whole world knows me and loves me and honours me as Pope Julius the Second.

(*as Alexander*) You? Pope? O disgrace. O Holy Church in decay.

(*as Julius*) Disgrace yourself! You and all your illegitimate children.

(*as Alexander*) Holy Church believes in the family. I set an example.

(*as Julius*) Three times, you auctioned off your bastard daughter Lucrezia to the highest bidder. Three times!

(*as Alexander*) You bid often enough. But you're such a cheapskate…

(*as herself*) Oh, never mind. Excommunication is so boring.

> *She takes the puppets off her hands. From under the*
> *bed, a cat meows.*

Cleopatra?

ANGELA looks under the bed.

Cleo? Here, kitty kitty kitty. Here, puss. Puss puss puss. Come on. Come on.... All right, stay there. See if I care. Stupid cat.

Suddenly, GIOVANNI shoots through a hinged flap in the wall and lands right on ANGELA's bed.

GIOVANNI &
ANGELA   (*together*) Aaaah!

GIOVANNI whips the bed curtains closed.
ANGELA pulls them open.

ANGELA   Who are you? What are you doing in my bed? Come on, speak up.

GIOVANNI   A thousand pardons, *principessa*, I—

ANGELA   I'm not a princess, I'm a countess.

GIOVANNI   *Contessa*. A thousand pardons.

ANGELA   You said that before. You scared Cleopatra.

GIOVANNI   Who?

ANGELA   My kittycat.

GIOVANNI   Really, I must go.

ANGELA   Stop.

GIOVANNI   I can't.

ANGELA   I'll scream. The guard will come in and kill you.

GIOVANNI   And get blood all over these elegant sheets? Please reconsider.

Beat.

ANGELA   (*loud*) Help!

GIOVANNI   No! Shhh.

GUARD   (*off*) *Contessa*?

GIOVANNI draws his dagger.

ANGELA	(*louder*) Help!
	GIOVANNI offers the dagger to ANGELA.
GIOVANNI	Please!
	ANGELA takes the dagger.
ANGELA	(*to the offstage GUARD*) Never mind, Francesco. It's all right. Cleopatra just scratched me again.
GUARD	(*off*) *Grazie, contessa.*
ANGELA	Thank you, Francesco.
GIOVANNI	He owes you his life.
ANGELA	And you owe me yours. Here.
	ANGELA puts GIOVANNI's dagger on the bed.
GIOVANNI	That's better.
ANGELA	I know you.
GIOVANNI	You do?
ANGELA	Captain Giovanni.
GIOVANNI	Yes. But how?—
ANGELA	You certainly get around. I was in the Vatican not long ago, watching your little *tête-à-tête* on the terrace. Giovanni the moth meets Lucrezia the flame.
GIOVANNI	*Contessa—*
ANGELA	And here you are in Ferrara. I see you've been beaten. Did she do it herself? Did you enjoy it?
GIOVANNI	Not much, no.
ANGELA	Come and play with me.
GIOVANNI	Play?
ANGELA	Play. Here.

> *She gives him the puppet representing Pope*
> *Alexander VI and puts the one representing Pope*
> *Julius II on her own hand.*

GIOVANNI That's… that's Pope Julius!

ANGELA Yes. And who's that?

GIOVANNI Borgia.

ANGELA So that's the cast. Here's the situation. The two old enemies are arguing. I'll start. Ready?

GIOVANNI I have to go!

ANGELA Not until I say so. (*continuing, as Julius*) I curse you, Borgia! I curse you in your shroud. May your moth-eaten ghost suffer through the ages as upright Christians piss on your reputation over and over and over again. No one will ever pray to you.

GIOVANNI (*as Alexander*) What? I'll never be a saint? Never see my name in gold on the calendar?

ANGELA (*as herself, laughing*) That's good! That's very good.

(*as Julius*) No calendar. No feast day. No stained-glass windows. No respect. Ever! Ha ha ha ha ha.

GIOVANNI (*as Alexander*) May big fat spiders squat on your ugly face.

ANGELA (*as Julius*) Ewww! Even as we speak, big fat worms are eating your little tiny penis.

GIOVANNI (*as Alexander*) Ow! Shut up!

ANGELA (*as Julius*) You shut up!

> *GIOVANNI starts to snarl and growl. His foot*
> *paws the floor. ANGELA does the same. Finally,*
> *"Julius" attacks. He grabs "Alexander" in his*
> *jaws, and they struggle, making horrible noises.*
> *Suddenly "Julius" pulls the "Alexander" puppet*
> *off GIOVANNI's hand, and flings him into a corner.*
> *GIOVANNI takes ANGELA's arm—with "Julius"*
> *on it—and holds it up. He bows.*

ANGELA   I win! I win!

GIOVANNI   All hail the holy victor, Pope Julius the Second.

ANGELA   You're fun to play with.

GIOVANNI   Next time I'll choose the game. For now, I'll just
            say farewell to the beautiful and charming and
            gifted Countess Angela DiGhilini.

ANGELA   I never told you my name.

GIOVANNI   You are young, you are bold, you live in the Duke's
            palace, there's a secret passage between…. Logic
            makes it clear who you are.

ANGELA   Captain Giovanni—

GIOVANNI   At your service.

ANGELA   At my service, at the service of every young
            noblewoman in the country. Half the girls in Italy
            whisper tales of Captain Giovanni, the famous
            bastard lover. And here you are, in the nice warm
            flesh. Isn't *Donna* Lucrezia a little old for you?

GIOVANNI   Ah, *contessa*, forgive me. I don't have time. And
            I like to take time.

ANGELA   I don't recall asking you—

GIOVANNI   Your beautiful eyes asked me.

ANGELA   Oh, ick.

GIOVANNI   And I would say yes, except that duty calls, and
            I must go. How do I get out of here without having
            to kill the guard?

ANGELA   Under the bed. There's a hatch.

GIOVANNI   Where does it lead?

ANGELA   Outside. You won't be seen.

GIOVANNI   You've taken this exit yourself?

ANGELA   I'm a night person.

            *She takes GIOVANNI's hand and slides his thumb
            into her mouth. He responds, then pulls back.*

GIOVANNI   I don't want to leave, but I must. May I?

ANGELA   When we want something, we say…?

GIOVANNI   Please?

ANGELA   All right. Just this once.

GIOVANNI   If we meet again, I hope it is in this world.

ANGELA   Mmmm.

> *He dives under the bed. We hear the hatch open.*

GIOVANNI   (*off*) Hello, kitty. Puss puss puss…

> *Under the bed, the cat snarls and scratches him.*

Ow! Fuck!

> *The hatch closes with a bang. ANGELA giggles.*
> *Lights down.*

ACT I

Scene 8

> *Ferrara. A dungeon in Alfonso's palace. Lights up*
> *as Sister BIBIANA wheels in a cart laden with*
> *scientific apparatus and two covered baskets.*
> *ANGELA is with her.*

ANGELA   I don't want to!

BIBIANA   You don't have to want to. You just have to. The
Duke insists. And I know you want to please the
Duke.

ANGELA   I please Alfonso just fine as I am.

BIBIANA   Then make this an occasion for grace. Yes, there
is grace even for the excommunicated. Here's how
it works: I teach you science. You suffer. You offer
up your suffering to God. God is pleased. So am
I. Now pay attention.

> *During the following, BIBIANA pulls snakes one by one out of one basket, milks their venom into a beaker, then drops them into the other basket.*

ANGELA   Snakes. Ugh!

BIBIANA   Come on, Jezebel. Spit for Mama. You give me venom, I'll give you a nice mouse.

ANGELA   Mice. Ugh!

BIBIANA   Where's your brother? Judas? Oh, there you are.

ANGELA   You have really ugly children.

BIBIANA   You mind your manners, young lady, or I'll give you something to read.

ANGELA   Reading. Bleah. What a waste of time.

BIBIANA   Think so? Then let me tell you a story.

> *BIBIANA searches the dungeon and finds a dead rat.*

Imagine that this rat is a bear. A big mama bear. Back before you were born, every so often I'd have some peasants catch one and chain her over there. No food, just water. After a week, Mama was famished. Then I'd take raw meat, to which I'd add this

> *She shows ANGELA some deadly nightshade.*

ANGELA   What's that?

BIBIANA   Deadly nightshade. We call it *belladonna*. Pure poison. Tastes nasty, acts fast. We wanted to improve its flavour and slow down its effect.

ANGELA   Slow it down? Why?

BIBIANA   You don't want some poor fool writhing in agony at the dinner table. Tends to stop conversation. And you do want to leave enough time for last rites. We are Christians. Now this is how we reached our goal.

> *BIBIANA makes the rat "growl."*

Signora Bear smells the meat. Don't you, Mama? Dinner's almost ready. Say your prayers.

The rat "growls" again.

Amen—*Eccolà*. Death tartare—The famished bear would gobble up the poisoned meat. She'd tremble, then whine, then collapse. I'd tie a rope to her leg, run the rope through a pulley hung on that hook over there, then tug on it until she was hanging upside down. With her last breath, she'd vomit a golden liquid, which I'd catch in a silver bowl.

ANGELA   I'm sure that tasted much better.

BIBIANA   Not the golden liquid itself. I'd just scrape off the foam that rose to the top. It dried into a sparkling white powder. Cantarella. Pretty name, isn't it? The famous poison of the Borgias.

ANGELA   Then why do you need those snakes?

BIBIANA   Well, milady, back then we needed a lot of poison. We killed the mama bears faster than the papa bears made baby bears, and soon the forests of Italy had no bears left.

ANGELA   That was stupid.

BIBIANA   Yes, it was. So we prayed to God for guidance. And lo! Our prayers were answered. A few months after Cardinal Rodrigo Borgia was elected Pope, Christopher Columbus came back from the New World. He brought the Pope a present. Snakes.

ANGELA   And now you milk their babies?

BIBIANA   Correct. Complete this sentence: snakes are better than bears, because…?

ANGELA   Um… because… snakes breed faster.

BIBIANA   Very good. Why is that better?

ANGELA   Um… because… you get more venom in less time.

BIBIANA   Excellent!

ANGELA   What does any of this have to do with reading?

BIBIANA	I'm glad you asked. Tell me the truth: would you ever have figured out that you could use a bear as a poison refinery?
ANGELA	No.
BIBIANA	Neither would I. But somebody did, and wrote down the recipe. Somebody else found the recipe in the Vatican library, misfiled in the cookbook section.
ANGELA	Who?
BIBIANA	Someone who reads.
ANGELA	*Donna* Lucrezia.
BIBIANA	Right again.

ANGELA finds one of the snakes in her bodice.

ANGELA	Sister!
BIBIANA	Marco! There you are!
ANGELA	Get this thing off me!
BIBIANA	Marco Polo, you bad boy.
ANGELA	Crush his head.
BIBIANA	I will not. Oh, now you've hurt his feelings. Poor baby, so lovely and smooth. Here, kiss and make up.
ANGELA	Yaaa!
BIBIANA	Oh, don't be such a child.

ALFONSO strides in. He has a whip.

| ALFONSO | I swore that Giovanni bastard, Giovanni scum, Giovanni tin soldier of Pope Julius Pig, would not leave my palace alive. I poisoned him. But Giovanni escaped. From death. From Ferrara. From me. |
| BIBIANA | He's alive? |

ALFONSO	I promised God that Giovanni would die today. Someone has made me a liar. An excommunicated liar.
ANGELA	*Donna* Lucrezia.
ALFONSO	No doubt. But how?
ANGELA	Ask her.
ALFONSO	I have. Repeatedly. She just laughs.
ANGELA	Torture her.
ALFONSO	No.
ANGELA	Why not?
BIBIANA	Because he loves her.
ANGELA	He loves me.
ALFONSO	I will deal with Lucrezia and Giovanni in good time. And with any co-conspirators.... What have we here? Reptiles.
ANGELA	You want me to learn science.
ALFONSO	I do?
ANGELA	That's what Sister says.
ALFONSO	I see. Perhaps the teacher needs a lesson more than the student.
ANGELA	Yes!
BIBIANA	No!
ALFONSO	Then why do you want to teach the contessa science?
BIBIANA	She's a natural.
ALFONSO	Really? So you're training her to poison me?
BIBIANA	No, sir! Never!
ALFONSO	Dear Sister Bibiana. I want to believe you. Now, I poisoned Captain Giovanni. Why didn't he die?
BIBIANA	I don't know.

ALFONSO	Why don't you know? You know everything else. You made the poison. You make all our poison these days, don't you? Including the last batch? Why didn't Giovanni die?
BIBIANA	*Don* Alfonso, I did everything the way I always do it. Milk the snakes, mix the venom with these chemicals, dry it out, fill *Donna* Lucrezia's ring. That's it.
ALFONSO	Sounds right to me. And yet, Giovanni lives. Such a mystery.
BIBIANA	Are you sure you gave him the right dose?
ALFONSO	Oh, so now it's my fault. Sister Bibiana, put your hand in the basket.
ANGELA	That won't punish her. She does that all the time.
BIBIANA	*Don* Alfonso, please, I didn't mean to suggest—
ALFONSO	Punish her? No, I just never get tired of seeing it. You know all these snakes by name, right? And they know how gentle you are with them. So they won't hurt you, will they? Put your hand in the basket.

BIBIANA does so.

ANGELA	How can she stand to do that?
ALFONSO	I couldn't do it. They'd bite me. But they won't bite her. Will they, Sister?

Suddenly, ALFONSO cracks the whip, which curls around the basket. He jerks it. Twice. BIBIANA shrieks in pain and pulls her bleeding hand out of the basket. There's a snake attached.

ANGELA	Alfonso!
ALFONSO	Oh, dear.

ALFONSO detaches the snake, drops it on the floor, and steps on it.

BIBIANA	Murderer. Murderer.

BIBIANA collapses.

ALFONSO   We'll see—Outside there! Let her in!

LUCREZIA enters as though she has been forcibly kept outside.

LUCREZIA   Alfonso! What have you done?

BIBIANA   My snakes.

ALFONSO   Giovanni should be dead, but he's alive. Therefore, you must have given him an antidote. Now, I want that antidote, and I want the truth. So, you can watch your oldest friend die, and keep your secret, or you can reveal it and save her life.

BIBIANA   *Madonna?*

LUCREZIA   Bibiana—

BIBIANA   Is there really an antidote?

LUCREZIA   Yes.

ALFONSO   Aha!

BIBIANA   May I please have some?

LUCREZIA   Bibiana, I—Angela! In my bedchamber, the armoire, upper shelf, at the very back, the little box. Get it. Hurry!

ANGELA runs out.

BIBIANA   O God, I am heartily sorry for offending thee—

She coughs up blood.

LUCREZIA   Alfonso, get a priest.

ALFONSO   From where? They all ran away when we were excommunicated. And Cardinal Vincenzo's gone hunting.

BIBIANA   No priest?

LUCREZIA   Bibiana, it's all right. I'll hear your confession.

ALFONSO   What?

LUCREZIA	Like the early Church, before priests were invented. Now get out, Alfonso. The confessional is sealed.
ALFONSO	Nice try. I'm staying right here.
BIBIANA	Forgive me, Lord, for I have sinned.
LUCREZIA	How?
BIBIANA	I—I can't remember them all.
LUCREZIA	God can.
BIBIANA	I remember one.
LUCREZIA	Do you repent?
BIBIANA	Oh God!
LUCREZIA	I'll take that as a yes. You are forgiven. This agony is your penance.
BIBIANA	Not yet, *madonna*. I lied to you once. Only once. Do you remember Perotto?
ALFONSO	Who?
LUCREZIA	Be quiet!—Yes, of course I remember. What about him?
BIBIANA	Perotto's—legacy. I can't feel my legs. Where's Angela?
LUCREZIA	On her way. You were saying?
BIBIANA	Perotto's legacy…. Cold. I can't feel… so cold. His legacy… did not die. I saved him.
LUCREZIA	You—
BIBIANA	Saved him. Sturdy little boy. Big eyes. He smiled at me and peed on my habit. I sent him to a village on the seacoast. Kept… souvenir. Red silk… here… aah!

BIBIANA coughs up more blood, then dies.

ALFONSO	Sweet Jesus.
LUCREZIA	Your sins are washed away. Rest now. Rest.

ALFONSO   Your antidote could have saved her.

LUCREZIA   No. I gave it all to Giovanni.

ALFONSO   But you sent Angela—

LUCREZIA   She didn't need to be here. Neither did you. But you insisted. Happy now?

> *LUCREZIA searches BIBIANA's habit and finds a red silk scarf, torn in half. ANGELA runs in, carrying a small box.*

ANGELA   Here's the box. But it's locked. Oh, God. Is she?—

LUCREZIA   Dead? Yes. Don't blame yourself. I'm sure you ran as fast as you could.

ALFONSO   Angela, it's not your fault. I'll tell you—

ANGELA   Tell me nothing! You killed her! You made me watch and—

> *ANGELA grabs the whip from ALFONSO and lashes him with it.*

ALFONSO   Angela! Stop it. Stop—Ow! Get—You don't realize what—Ow!

> *ALFONSO runs out. ANGELA bursts into racking sobs and runs out another way. LUCREZIA looks at the red silk scarf.*

LUCREZIA   "Perotto's legacy." Our son, Perotto, yours and mine! Alive! And he and I.... Oh, my God.

> *Lights down.*

> *END OF ACT I*

ACT II

Scene 1

Lights up on BIBIANA's corpse on a bier.
LUCREZIA prays silently. ANGELA talks to the
body.

ANGELA   You tried to teach me about sin. Pride. Gluttony.
            Sloth. Anger. Greed. Envy. Lust. Despair.
            Oppressing the poor. Defrauding workers of their
            wages. "The sin of the cities of the plain." What
            does that mean? You'd never tell me. "When you're
            older," you said. I'm older now!—Sister Bibiana,
            I'm sorry you're dead.

LUCREZIA   Amen.

ANGELA   Why would God listen to us?

LUCREZIA   Do you doubt it?

ANGELA   We're excommunicated.

LUCREZIA   Not by God. By the Pope.

ANGELA   The Pope speaks for God the Father.

LUCREZIA   I'm a Pope's daughter. I know the difference
            between one father and another.

ANGELA   God let Bibiana die. God's deaf. There is no God!

LUCREZIA   Well, make up your mind.

ANGELA   I was mean to her.

LUCREZIA   Yes, you were.

ANGELA   Stop attacking me!

LUCREZIA   Sorry.

ANGELA   I'm going to hell. I know it.

LUCREZIA   Why would you want to do that?

ANGELA   I don't want to!

LUCREZIA	Then don't.
ANGELA	It's not up to me.
LUCREZIA	Who is it up to?
ANGELA	God.
LUCREZIA	The one who doesn't exist?
ANGELA	I… I don't know.
LUCREZIA	I see.
ANGELA	I could… I could give Alfonso back to you.
LUCREZIA	God might see that as a sacrifice. I'm not sure whose.
ANGELA	It's a good deed. You're married.
LUCREZIA	Don't you want him any more?
ANGELA	Don't you?
LUCREZIA	I don't have to want him. We're married.
ANGELA	He makes my flesh crawl.
LUCREZIA	Yes, I've seen your flesh crawl. All over him.
ANGELA	You slept with that soldier.
LUCREZIA	That's different. Different.
ANGELA	Was it worth it?
LUCREZIA	None of your business.
ANGELA	I'm never getting married.
LUCREZIA	No, you don't stand on ceremony, do you?
ANGELA	Don't pretend you care.
LUCREZIA	My poor old Bibiana.
ANGELA	Crocodile tears.
LUCREZIA	Crocodile teeth. Beware.
ANGELA	Did you ever love him?

LUCREZIA Who?

ANGELA Alfonso.

LUCREZIA That's between him and me.

ANGELA He says, he married you for political reasons.

LUCREZIA Yes. It was Alfonso's father's idea. Duke Ercole. He told Alfonso, "Marry Lucrezia. We need the Borgias more than they need us." Alfonso said no, he couldn't bear the disgrace. I'd already been married twice. His father said, "Fine. If you're too sensitive to marry Lucrezia Borgia, you're too sensitive to rule Ferrara. So I'll marry her. She'll give me babies. They will inherit Ferrara. You will get nothing." Alfonso caved in. But he was "too busy" to come to Rome for our wedding. Sent his brother as a stand-in. Some wedding day! I was married, by proxy, to a man I'd never even met! And yet Alfonso was in Rome.

ANGELA He was?

LUCREZIA According to Bibiana.

ANGELA Spying on you?

LUCREZIA He does that. As you well know. He'd even ordered his brother Ippolito—

ANGELA The cardinal?

LUCREZIA Yes. Alfonso ordered his brother to try to seduce me so Alfonso would be off the hook. I disappointed both of them. I arrived here a week later. Alfonso must have liked what he saw; he made sure that the entire household staff eavesdropped on us the afternoon I got here, that night and all the next day. Witnesses to the noisy and extended consummation of the glorious union between the powerful Borgia and the noble d'Este families, joined forever, or as long as forever lasts in Italy, amen.

> *ANGELA begins to cry. LUCREZIA hesitates, then touches her. ANGELA grabs LUCREZIA and holds*

her fiercely.
Lights down.

ACT II

Scene 2

Ferrara. LUCREZIA's bedchamber. Outside, wind
and rain. Lights up on LUCREZIA, dreaming. She
wears a nightgown.

LUCREZIA   Are you there…? Are you ever there…? Speak up,
O great Absence in the sky. Lord, talk to me!
I made love with my own son. If he is my son. And
I hope to you he is. But one red silk scarf is like
another. Maybe he's someone else's child. He's
gone. I'll never see him again. That's punishment
enough. But maybe my child lives, thank you, O
silent God, for your blessing. Your curse. Which is
it…? Thunder. Lightning. Rain. It's warm, it's cold,
it means nothing…. Lord? Can you hear me? Hear
me now! My child was dead. Bibiana brought me
a little grey corpse and said he was mine. I held
him. I mourned him. Who was he? It's raining.
God's not home. Maybe he's out in the rain. I am
alone. I think forever. What prayer is there for
that…? Giovanni. I wanted him. Hot, tight flesh,
a young man's *braggadocio*, sweet, more stamina
than finesse, he might be my son, I am so proud.
Blessèd am I among women, for I have had my
child inside me twice, coming out and going in!—
Curse me, Lord, I don't care. Your curse is rain. So
hide, you coward God. Tomorrow I'm coming to
find you. Wherever you are.

The candles flicker. GIOVANNI appears behind
LUCREZIA. Aware that something is different,
LUCREZIA hesitates, then crosses herself.

Amen.

> *She blows out the candles and gets into bed.*
> *GIOVANNI sits on the bed. After a moment,*
> *LUCREZIA sits up.*

Giovanni! How did you get?—Why?

GIOVANNI   I had to. I know it's not safe. I don't care.

LUCREZIA   (*to God*) Is this your answer…? Giovanni! I thought I'd never see you again. But you have to go. You're in more danger now than ever.

GIOVANNI   You smell so good. I want to inhale you, touch you, Lucrezia!—

> *LUCREZIA scrambles out of bed.*

LUCREZIA   No!—We can't. It's wrong. You can't imagine. Please go. Please.

GIOVANNI   Look at me, Lucrezia.

LUCREZIA   Giovanni, no!

GIOVANNI   Yes. Yes. Yes.

> *GIOVANNI brings out his red scarf and with it,*
> *draws LUCREZIA to him. He kisses her.*
> *LUCREZIA responds, then pulls away. With the*
> *scarf, he pulls her back, drawing her toward the bed.*

LUCREZIA   God, where are you…? I can't…! Ahh! It's my sin. Mine. Not his.

> *The bed curtains close. Darkness. The sounds of*
> *great passion. Outside, the wind and rain increase.*
> *Lights down.*

ACT II

Scene 3

> *Dawn. LUCREZIA's bedchamber. Behind the*
> *curtains, the couple in bed stirs, sighs. LUCREZIA*
> *flings open the curtains, then turns to her partner.*

It's ALFONSO! Shocked, LUCREZIA jumps out of bed.

ALFONSO   Come back here. I want more. You were inspired.

LUCREZIA   What?

ALFONSO   Last night. You were inspired, you inspired me. Now come here.

LUCREZIA   Alfonso, no. Please. I... I don't know why, but this morning I feel almost... virginal.

ALFONSO   Virginal!

He roars with laughter. LUCREZIA laughs, too.

LUCREZIA   It's even funnier than it sounds.

ALFONSO   Oh, God. That's the second-best way to start the day. Now for the best way...

LUCREZIA   Alfonso... this scarf... Alfonso, Giovanni might be my son. I might have slept with my own child.

ALFONSO   So?

LUCREZIA   Don't you care?

ALFONSO   It's between you and God. I know you. You'll spend the rest of your life eating your heart out: "Is he or isn't he?" Oh, Lucrezia, look at that glorious sunrise! I haven't seen one in a long time.

LUCREZIA   Not from my window.

ALFONSO   God damn! I've got a feeling—I'm going to try to negotiate with Cardinal Vincenzo one last time.

LUCREZIA   Alfonso! He was here last night.

ALFONSO   Vincenzo?

LUCREZIA   Giovanni.

ALFONSO   Don't be silly. I was here then and I'm here now. You can't pick a fight with me, Lucrezia. Not after last night.

LUCREZIA   I was with Giovanni. Heart and mind and soul and body. And oh, I know the difference!

ALFONSO   Whose son is he? Your brother's? Your father's?

LUCREZIA   A man I loved. A man I'll never forget. A better
man than you!

> *ALFONSO grabs the red silk scarf and twists it
> around LUCREZIA's neck.*

ALFONSO   Bitch!

LUCREZIA   Kill me! My soul will never die!

> *Beat. He lets her go.*

ALFONSO   You kill me.

LUCREZIA   Don't you want me? Don't you want me now? I am
your wife. Your virgin bride. Here I am. Come and
get me.

> *ALFONSO does not move.*
> *Lights down.*

ACT II

Scene 4

> *The ghost of SISTER BIBIANA appears, wearing
> angel wings. She has a snake with her; it has angel
> wings too.*

BIBIANA   (*to us*) Surprised? Me too! I thought I was headed
for the eternal Pit, then straight up Satan's rectum.
But God's grace is infinite. I'm in heaven! And so is
Lilith. She bit me, that nasty Duke killed her, but
now we're reunited after so much pain. Enough
about me. A lot has happened since we saw you
last, hasn't it, baby?

Despite Alfonso's optimism, he and Cardinal
Vincenzo could not come to an agreement. So
Vincenzo goes back to Rome, and the Pope's army
prepares to attack Ferrara. Meanwhile, for other
reasons, the King of France decides to attack the

Pope. Alfonso offers the French army free passage through Ferrara and his help in capturing the city of Bologna. But when they take Bologna, Alfonso keeps the French troops outside the city just long enough for him to seize the cathedral and loot it himself. He only takes one thing: a big bronze statue of Pope Julius. That's right, the one by Michelangelo.

Alfonso takes the statue to a foundry, where he has it melted down and recast into a cannon. He christens it by urinating on it. Really, he's not a very pious man. He names the cannon *"La Giulia,"* thus womanizing the Pope's name, and sends it to the Pope as a gift. His message says, "Holiness, kiss your twin sister. Like you, she belches gas, makes lots of noise, and—miracle of miracles!—throws her big balls all over creation."

Well! The Pope just explodes. He yells out, "Begone from Italy, French scum! Begone from Italy, Alfonso d'Este!" And then he has a stroke—babump, babump, babump—and dies. I saw it all from up here. Great seats. Look! White smoke! They've elected a new Pope!—Gotta go. I'll be seeing some of you soon. Maybe. Come on, Lilith.

Lights down.

ACT II

Scene 5

GIOVANNI's lodgings. Lights up on GIOVANNI, looking out the window, stroking his red silk scarf. We can see light—torches, bonfires, fireworks—and we can hear shouts of "Viva il Papa!" answered by more shouts of "Evviva!" Suddenly, LUCREZIA bursts in. She is wearing BIBIANA's habit and cross.

LUCREZIA   There you are! Thank God.

GIOVANNI   Sister Bib—*Donna* Lucrezia! Wha?—

LUCREZIA   Giovanni, I have to—

GIOVANNI   Did anyone see you? Rome is still—

LUCREZIA   Dangerous. I know. But I had to come here.

GIOVANNI   You have to come here and kiss me. Habit or not.

LUCREZIA   No, I—

    He kisses her thoroughly. She breaks away, gasping.

    Wait—

GIOVANNI   Wait? Yes. Right. We'll take it slow. We haven't done that yet. Slow. Imagine.

    He throws the scarf around her and draws her to him.

LUCREZIA   Giovanni, stop. I have something important to tell you.

GIOVANNI   First things first.

LUCREZIA   Listen to me! Giovanni, you need to know.

GIOVANNI   Know what?

LUCREZIA   I know... I think I know who you are.

GIOVANNI   You do know who I am. More than any living soul.

LUCREZIA   I'm talking about your parents. Your real parents.

GIOVANNI   How could you know that?

LUCREZIA   Oh, I could.

GIOVANNI   Then tell me. Tell me!

LUCREZIA   When I was a child, Pope Alexander—my father— asked me if I would do him a favour. I said yes, Papa, of course. A few weeks later, I was married, in the Vatican, by my father, to Giovanni Sforza. My husband was 26. I was 13.

GIOVANNI   This isn't news. Your husband ignored you. You ran away from him and took refuge in a convent. So?

LUCREZIA   There are things you don't know! I refused to see my father. But after awhile, I got restless. My father sent his chamberlain, a man named Perotto, to bribe me with new clothes, new jewels, news of the latest Vatican intrigues. Perotto was witty, and handsome, and kind. Then my father decided he didn't need the Sforza alliance after all. My brother Cesare—

GIOVANNI   Cesare Borgia. They say that you and he—

LUCREZIA   Hush. I know what they say. Cesare gave my husband a choice: say he was impotent, or get his throat cut. My husband was dull, but not stupid. He swore in public that he'd never been able to consummate our marriage. I came to Rome and swore the same thing to a panel of cardinals. They annulled our marriage and proclaimed me *virgo intacta*.

GIOVANNI   Were you?

LUCREZIA   What do you think?

GIOVANNI   How corrupt can the Church get?

LUCREZIA   I hope that's a rhetorical question. There was one small problem: I was pregnant. Perotto begged for his life but Cesare stabbed him in the heart.

GIOVANNI   Your brother murdered your lover.

LUCREZIA   I went back to the convent. I had my baby. They told me it died.

GIOVANNI   I'm sorry. Perhaps it was for the best.

LUCREZIA   That's what they said. Anyway, I was free, until my father needed another political alliance.

GIOVANNI   What does any of this have to do with me?

            LUCREZIA pulls her half of the scarf from her habit.

LUCREZIA   Here.

> *GIOVANNI fits the two scarves together. They match.*

GIOVANNI   Where did you get this? Where are my parents? What have you done to my parents?

LUCREZIA   Giovanni—

ANGELA   (*off*) Giovanni?

GIOVANNI   Who's that?

LUCREZIA   Why, it's little Angela. A long way from home.

GIOVANNI   We're not finished, you and I.

LUCREZIA   No, we're not.

ANGELA   (*off*) Giovanni, where are you?

GIOVANNI   Up here!

> *LUCREZIA hides behind a curtain. ANGELA enters. She still has ALFONSO's whip.*

ANGELA   Giovanni. At last. Hold me. Hold me tight.

GIOVANNI   *Contessa*—

ANGELA   No, Giovanni. Not *contessa*. Angela. For you. Angela.

> *She kisses him avidly.*

GIOVANNI   You honour me.

ANGELA   It was awful. So awful. Now she's dead. I thought I wanted her to die but I didn't, but Alfonso thought I did, and he—

GIOVANNI   Who? Who are we talking about?

ANGELA   Sister Bibiana.

GIOVANNI   Sister Bibiana is dead?

ANGELA   Poisoned. Lucrezia sent me to find an antidote, but I couldn't open it, I couldn't open it, and Bibiana's dead, and I need you.

LUCREZIA reveals herself.

LUCREZIA   Hello, Angela.

ANGELA   *Donna* Lucrezia!

LUCREZIA   Not enough you seduce my husband, you have to throw yourself after my… after Giovanni, too?

ANGELA   It's over with Alfonso. I want Giovanni now. (*to GIOVANNI*) You have to choose. Her or me.

LUCREZIA   Angela, understand me clearly. You will never have Giovanni. I forbid it.

ANGELA   She killed Bibiana.

GIOVANNI   I thought you said the Duke—

ANGELA   Ask her!

GIOVANNI   Is that true?

LUCREZIA   In a way. I gave you the antidote.

GIOVANNI   She was my friend. And yours!

LUCREZIA   Her death saved your life.

GIOVANNI   Did my mother's death save yours?

LUCREZIA   Who says your mother is dead?

GIOVANNI   Is she alive? Tell me. Is my father alive? Where is he? Where is my mother?

ALFONSO enters.

ALFONSO   Closer than you think.

GIOVANNI grabs his sword.

ANGELA   Alfonso!

GIOVANNI   Does everybody know where I live?

ALFONSO   Put the weapon away, boy. You won't need it.

GIOVANNI   I'll decide that.

ALFONSO   As you wish.

LUCREZIA   I wish you'd stop following me.

ANGELA   He was following me.

ALFONSO   I have news.

GIOVANNI   What have you two done with my parents?

ALFONSO   The excommunication is over.

LUCREZIA   What?

ANGELA   Thank God.

ALFONSO   In his wisdom, the new Pope has lifted the interdiction on Ferrara and the excommunication on us.

LUCREZIA   What did that cost you?

ALFONSO   He did it for the good of the Church. It says so right here.

> *ALFONSO shows her a scroll.*

LUCREZIA   So I see. And are we still allied with the French?

ALFONSO   What French? We're Italian, and proud of it.

LUCREZIA   I thought so.

ANGELA   Giovanni, run away with me.

LUCREZIA   That's not going to happen.

ALFONSO   No, it isn't. You're coming home where you belong.

ANGELA   I am not.

ALFONSO   You have no say in the matter.

GIOVANNI   Oh, yes, she does.

> *He brandishes his sword.*

ALFONSO   We'll see.

> *He draws his sword.*

ANGELA   (*to ALFONSO*) Don't hurt him.

GIOVANNI   I won't.

ALFONSO   You won't be able to.

> *They duel. ALFONSO and GIOVANNI are rather evenly matched, and somewhat to the surprise of both, they are enjoying themselves.*

GIOVANNI   This is for Sister Bibiana.

ALFONSO   This is for *Donna* Lucrezia.

GIOVANNI   This is for *Donna* Angela.

ANGELA   I'm all wet.

ALFONSO   This is for my honour.

GIOVANNI   This is for my mother.

ALFONSO   Ah yes, your mother.

GIOVANNI   Where is she? Where is my mother?

LUCREZIA   Alfonso!—

ALFONSO   Right there, dear Giovanni, right there. Lucrezia Borgia is your mother.

> *Shocked, GIOVANNI drops his guard for a moment. ALFONSO wounds him and is about to run him through when LUCREZIA takes the stiletto from BIBIANA's cross and stabs ALFONSO in the arm, making him drop his sword. GIOVANNI is about to run ALFONSO through.*

LUCREZIA   Giovanni, no!

> *GIOVANNI turns his sword toward LUCREZIA.*

GIOVANNI   *Don* Alfonso has made an accusation. Is it true? Is it true?

LUCREZIA   Yes.

GIOVANNI   God forgive…. You knew this when we?—

LUCREZIA   No! Sister Bibiana showed me a stillborn baby and said he was mine. How was I to know? And then you mentioned a torn scarf, and Bibiana had one, and…

ANGELA   You slept with your own mother?

ALFONSO   Makes you think, doesn't it?

GIOVANNI   Your grace, I'm learning the hard way not to fish in another man's pond.

ALFONSO   Well, for what it's worth, you have lovely bait.

GIOVANNI   You're very kind.

ALFONSO   You'll do well, Giovanni Borgia.

GIOVANNI   Please don't call me that.

ALFONSO   Why not? You're certainly worthy of the name.

GIOVANNI   What was my father's name?

LUCREZIA   Caldes. Pedro Caldes. Everyone called him Perotto.

GIOVANNI   Caldes. I am Giovanni Caldes!

ALFONSO   You have powerful women behind you, Giovanni Caldes. And ahead of you, I imagine.

GIOVANNI   *Don* Alfonso, *Donna* Lucrezia, *Donna* Angela: I'm going to confession.

ANGELA   We can all go to confession now!

ALFONSO   Angela, stay.

ANGELA   No!

> *She brandishes the whip. ALFONSO cringes.*
> *ANGELA evades him and runs out the door.*

GIOVANNI   Mother?

LUCREZIA   Mother. Oh, Giovanni—

GIOVANNI   Mother, when you and *Don* Alfonso leave, please lock the door behind you.

> *GIOVANNI exits.*

ALFONSO   Well, my honour is satisfied, I suppose.

LUCREZIA   Then I claim a mother's honour. I'm pregnant.

ALFONSO   You're what? Whose is it?

LUCREZIA   Mine.

ALFONSO   No more games, Lucrezia. Who's the father?

LUCREZIA   What will you do if it's Giovanni's?

ALFONSO   Kill the little bastard.

LUCREZIA   Then thank God it's yours.

ALFONSO   Are you telling the truth?

LUCREZIA   Oh ye of little faith. It's yours, Alfonso. It's yours.

ALFONSO   That's more like it.

LUCREZIA   At least in public.

> *LUCREZIA smiles like Mona Lisa. Lights down slowly.*
>
> *END OF PLAY*

David Copelin

David has worked across the continent as a resident dramaturg in several not-for-profit theatres, as a theatre professor, and as a story consultant for Warner Bros. Pictures in New York. His adaptation of Alfred Jarry's *Ubu Roi* was staged by Allen MacInnes at the Shaw Festival in 1990. David's book *Practical Playwriting* (Boston: The Writer, Inc.) was published in 1998. From 1999 to 2003, David served as Artistic Director of ScriptLab. Trained at Yale Drama School, he has been a dramaturg for many individual playwrights through his scriptwriting seminars in Toronto and at Brock University. His short plays *Mind over Matter*, *Vandals*, *Quite Contrary*, and *A Clean Breast* have been produced in various venues. David is a voting member of the Dramatists Guild of America and the Playwrights Guild of Canada. He is also Vice-Chair of the Public Lending Right Commission in Ottawa and an adjudicator for Theatre Ontario. A founding member and former President of Literary Managers and Dramaturgs of the Americas, David is currently writing *The Rabbi of Ragged Ass Road*, a comic fantasy set in Yellowknife. He lives in Toronto.